1, 2 CORINTHIANS

BOOKS OF FAITH SERIES
Learner Session Guide

Ritva H. Williams

Minneapolis

1, 2 CORINTHIANS
Learner Session Guide

Books of Faith Series
Book of Faith Adult Bible Studies

Copyright © 2011 Augsburg Fortress. All rights reserved. Except for brief quotations in critical articles or reviews, no part of this book may be reproduced in any manner without prior written permission from the publisher. For more information, visit: www.augsburgfortress.org/copyrights or write to: Permissions, Augsburg Fortress, Box 1209, Minneapolis, MN 55440-1209.

 Book of Faith is an initiative of the
Evangelical Lutheran Church in America
God's work. Our hands.

For more information about the Book of Faith initiative, go to www.bookoffaith.org.

Scripture quotations, unless otherwise marked, are from New Revised Standard Version Bible, copyright © 1989 Division of Christian Education of the National Council of Churches of Christ in the United States of America. Used by permission. All rights reserved.

References to *ELW* are from *Evangelical Lutheran Worship* (Augsburg Fortress, 2006).

Web site addresses are provided in this resource for your use. These listings do not represent an endorsement of the sites by Augsburg Fortress, nor do we vouch for their content for the life of this resource.

ISBN: 978-1-4514-0143-1

Writer: Ritva H. Williams
Cover and interior design: Spunk Design Machine, spkdm.com
Typesetting: Timothy W. Larson, Minneapolis, MN

The paper used in this publication meets the minimum requirements of American National Standard for Information Sciences—Permanence of Paper for Printed Library Materials, ANSI Z329.48-1984.

Manufactured in the U.S.A.
14 13 12 11 1 2 3 4 5 6 7 8 9 10

CONTENTS

1 Whose Am I? — 5
1 Corinthians 1:1-30

2 What Then Am I? — 11
1 Corinthians 3:1—4:5

3 It's Not All about Me? — 16
1 Corinthians 6:12-20; 10:23-33

4 What Am I Good For? — 21
1 Corinthians 12:1-31

5 What Will I Be Ultimately? — 26
1 Corinthians 15:12-28, 35-58

6 How Do I Achieve This Glory? — 32
2 Corinthians 3:1—4:15

7 What Can I Do Here and Now? — 38
2 Corinthians 4:16—5:21

8 What Is My Response to God's Grace? — 43
2 Corinthians 8:1-15; 9:1-15

SESSION ONE

1 Corinthians 1:1-30

Learner Session Guide

Focus Statement

In baptism we are claimed by Christ for God.

Key Verse

[God] is the source of your life in Christ Jesus, who became for us wisdom from God, and righteousness and sanctification and redemption. 1 Corinthians 1:30

Whose Am I?

Focus Image

© Brendan Hunter / iStockphoto

Gather

Check-in

Take this time to connect or reconnect with the others in your group.

Pray

Blessed Lord God, you have caused the Holy Scriptures to be written for the nourishment of your people. Grant that we may hear them, read, mark, learn and inwardly digest them, that comforted by your promises, we may embrace and forever hold fast to the hope of eternal life, which you have given us in Jesus Christ, our Savior and Lord. Amen. (ELW, p. 72)

Focus Activity

In one minute or less, write down the names of persons or groups that claim you as theirs.

Session 1: 1 Corinthians 1:1-30   5

SESSION ONE

 Notes

Open Scripture

Read 1 Corinthians 1:1-30.

- What words or phrases caught your attention as you listened to this text?

- What people or situations were called to mind?

- What concerns were raised?

Join the Conversation

Literary Context

1. The first three verses of the session Scripture text make it clear that this is a letter written by the apostle Paul to the congregation he founded in Corinth. This was one of several congregations he established in cities scattered around the eastern end of the Mediterranean Sea. This letter is part of an ongoing long-distance relationship between Paul and members of the Corinthian church involving multiple letters, some of which have not survived (see 1 Corinthians 5:9; 7:1).

- Reading this letter is like listening in on one side of a telephone conversation. Based on what Paul says in 1 Corinthians 1, how would you describe his relationship with the church in Corinth? What seems to be happening in the congregation?

- Reread 1 Corinthians 1:2-9 and 1:26-31 and circle the words that Paul uses to describe the Corinthian congregation and its members. What are the characteristics of the church and its members? What or who is the source of these attributes? To whom do the people belong?

Notes

2. Wisdom is an important theme in the first two chapters of 1 Corinthians, where Paul contrasts God's wisdom with worldly wisdom.
- Look again at 1 Corinthians 1:17-31. What is wisdom? What is at the heart and center of God's wisdom, according to Paul?
- List some examples of worldly wisdom that are current in our culture today. How would they measure up against God's wisdom, as defined by Paul?

Historical Context

1. First Corinthians was written about five years after Paul planted the church in Corinth. This means that the first readers were relatively new Christians. They were still learning how to integrate faith with their previously held values, attitudes, and behavior. As first-century Greeks and Romans, they had been raised in a culture that placed a very high value on public honor and prestige deriving from social status. If one was not nobly born, well educated, or influential in society, one could acquire public prestige by associating with those who were. Working for, providing services to, and being seen in the company of high-status persons were ways that one could improve one's public image.
- Reread 1 Corinthians 1:10-16. How are these values evident in the behavior of the Corinthian Christians?
- To learn more about Apollos and Cephas, read Acts 18:24—19:1 and Galatians 1:18—2:14. What attributes of these men might have given them higher status than Paul, in the eyes of some Corinthian Christians?

2. Look at 1 Corinthians 1:26-31 again. According to Paul, what does God think of the Corinthian concern for honor and status among church members?
- What characteristics give church members status and importance today? How would Paul respond to these persons?

Lutheran Context

1. Martin Luther's teaching about the "theology of the cross" states that God comes to us in the very last place a reasonable person would think to look: as a baby sleeping in a manger, as a rough carpenter/healer/teacher from a backwoods region, and as a condemned rebel dying on a Roman cross.
- Reread 1 Corinthians 1:18-25. How does this passage support the theology of the cross?
- According to the theology of the cross, where are we most likely to find God present and actively at work in our communities? What

SESSION ONE

 **Notes**

implications does the theology of the cross have for how we ought to treat one another?

2. In the *Large Catechism*, Luther writes, "To be baptized in God's name is to be baptized not by human beings but by God himself. Although it is performed by human hands, it is nevertheless truly God's own act" (*The Book of Concord: The Confessions of the Evangelical Lutheran* Church, ed. Robert Kolb and Timothy J. Wengert [Fortress Press, 2000], 457.10).

- How does Luther's theology of the cross help us understand how God is active in human actions involving ordinary things like water?
- Consider Luther's claim that baptism is God's act. How does this change the way you think about baptism and what it means in your life?

Devotional Context

1. In the Focus Activity, you made a list of persons or groups that might claim you as their own. Review that list. Who is on your list and who is not? Why? If you had to rank the names on that list, which one would you put first? Based on Paul's message in 1 Corinthians 1:1-30, what might God have to say about your list? Whose are you? To whom do you really belong?

2. Look back at the Focus Image for the session. How does that image relate to Paul's message about baptism in 1 Corinthians 1:10-17? How might it resonate with Luther's understanding of baptism? How does it reflect your own experience of baptism?

3. Review the order for Holy Baptism in *Evangelical Lutheran Worship* (pp. 225–231). Reflect on how the words of the service might help us understand whose we are and to whom we belong.

- Draw or describe how you would picture doubt, then do the same for faith. What similarities and differences do you see between doubt and faith?
- Write or say a prayer asking and expecting God to give you the gift of wisdom.

Wrap-up

Be ready to look back over the work your group has done in this session.

Pray

We give you thanks, O God, that through water and the Holy Spirit you give us new birth, cleanse us from sin, and raise us to eternal life. Stir up in your people the gift of your Holy Spirit: the spirit of wisdom and understanding, the spirit of counsel and might, the spirit of knowledge and the fear of the Lord, the spirit of joy in your presence, both now and forever. Amen. (ELW, p. 237)

Extending the Conversation

Homework

1. Read the next session's Bible text: 1 Corinthians 3:1—4:5.

2. Begin each day by remembering your baptism and reminding yourself that you have been claimed by Christ for God, who is the source of your life and your salvation.

3. Become a "theologian of the cross" who intentionally seeks to be open to God's presence in the ordinary, hidden, and unexpected. Spend some time each day looking and listening for Christ in places where you would not normally expect to see, hear, or experience the divine. You might keep a daily journal in which you record your sightings of this God who is hidden in the ordinary.

Enrichment

1. If you want to read all of 1 and 2 Corinthians during this unit, read the following sections this week.
- Day 1: 1 Corinthians 1:1-17
- Day 2: 1 Corinthians 1:18-25
- Day 3: 1 Corinthians 1:26—2:5
- Day 4: 1 Corinthians 2:6-16
- Day 5: 1 Corinthians 3:1-9
- Day 6: 1 Corinthians 3:10-15
- Day 7: 1 Corinthians 3:16—4:5

2. Learn more about wisdom in the Bible and in the ancient world. You might read Job 28, Proverbs 1–2 and 8–9, or Ecclesiastes in the Bible; or search the Internet for information about ancient philosophers (literally "lovers of wisdom") such as Plato, Aristotle, the Epicureans, and the Stoics.

3. Watch the movie *Romero* (Paulist Productions, 1989) or *Bonhoeffer: Agent of Grace* (Vision Video, 2000). How is God's wisdom evident in these stories?

 Notes

SESSION ONE

 **Notes**

For Further Reading

Charles B. Cousar, *A Theology of the Cross: The Death of Jesus in the Pauline Letters* (Augsburg Fortress, 1990).

Douglas John Hall, "The Theology of the Cross: A Usable Past." Available at www.elca.org.

From Jesus to Christ: The First Christians. DVD and book available at www.shoppbs.org.

Robert Kolb, "Luther on the Theology of the Cross" *Lutheran Quarterly* 14 (2002): 443–466. Available at www.lutheranquarterly.com (previous issues, Winter 2002).

Martin E. Marty, *Baptism: A User's Guide* (Augsburg Fortress, 2008).

Kirsi Stjerna, *No Greater Jewel: Thinking about Baptism with Luther* (Augsburg Fortress, 2009).

SESSION TWO

1 Corinthians 3:1—4:5

Learner Session Guide

Focus Statement
We are all servants, laborers working together in God's field and on God's building, the temple. Each one of us is also part of God's field and temple that needs planting, watering, and building up.

Key Verse
For we are God's servants, working together; you are God's field, God's building. . . . Do you not know that you are God's temple and that God's Spirit dwells in you?
1 Corinthians 3:9, 16

What Then Am I?

 Focus Image

© Hilary Seselja / iStockphoto

Gather

Check-in
Take this time to connect or reconnect with the others in your group. Be ready to share new thoughts or insights about your last session.

Pray
Gracious and holy God, give us diligence to seek you, wisdom to perceive you, and patience to wait for you. Grant us, O God, a mind to meditate on you; eyes to behold you; ears to listen for your word; a heart to love you; and a life to proclaim you; through the power of the Spirit of Jesus Christ, our Savior and Lord. Amen. (ELW, p. 76)

Focus Activity
Look at the Focus Image and think about the people involved in your growth in faith. Who has helped to plant the seeds, water and nurture the soil, and so on?

SESSION TWO

 **Notes**

Open Scripture

Read 1 Corinthians 3:1—4:5.

- What words or phrases caught your attention as you listened to this text?

- How would you describe the tone of this passage? How does it make you feel?

- What issues were raised?

Join the Conversation

Literary Context

1. Human beings label each other and call each other names (for example, darling or jerk) as a way of evaluating each other positively or negatively. In his desire to correct the behavior of church members, Paul attaches a number of labels to them.

- Reread 1 Corinthians 3:1-4 and circle or underline the different ways that Paul refers to the Corinthian Christians. What effect would these labels have on the hearers? What effect would these labels have on you if they came from a respected mentor?

2. A metaphor is a figure of speech that transfers meanings from one concept to another through comparison or resemblance (for example, God's Word is a lamp). In 1 Corinthians 3:5—4:1, Paul uses a number of metaphors to clarify the role of church leaders.

- Identify the metaphors in this text and the areas of everyday life from which Paul draws them.

- How well do these metaphors help you respond to the question, "What then am I?" How well do they help you understand your role in the life of your congregation? What other metaphors would you use?

3. In ancient Greek, as in many modern languages, there were different words for "you" (singular) and "you" (plural). Throughout Paul's letter to the Corinthians, he uses the plural form of the word.

- How does this affect the meaning of 1 Corinthians 3:16-17? What is Paul saying about the church as a whole?
- What evidence do you see today that the Holy Spirit resides in the church—the assembly of the baptized?

Historical Context

1. In session 1, we learned that ancient Greek and Roman societies were very status conscious, giving much honor and prestige to those who were nobly born, well educated, and holders of important public offices. Ordinary people competed for social status by boasting of their connections to such prestigious persons. These values and attitudes were reflected in the Corinthian church as cliques formed around leaders, and members argued over the relative merits and status of the persons who had been instrumental in bringing them to faith and/or baptizing them. The result was "jealousy and quarreling" (1 Corinthians 3:3).

- Identify who, according to Paul, should get the credit for bringing the Corinthians to faith, baptizing them, and building up their congregation.
- Reread 1 Corinthians 3:3; 3:12-15; and 4:3-5. Discuss how church leaders will be evaluated and by whom. How would Paul's advice affect the way the Corinthian Christians treat their leaders and each other?

2. Consider to what extent Paul's teaching on this subject is still countercultural—still contrary to the wisdom of this world (3:18-19). Discuss whether our contemporary values encourage us to see our leaders and ourselves as servants and stewards.

Lutheran Context

1. Lutheran theology upholds the "priesthood of the baptized," sometimes called the "priesthood of all believers." As Martin Luther explained, all who are baptized and believe in Christ are priests as stated in 1 Peter 2:9, and so are worthy to pray for, teach, and minister to one another, even if all do not do so publicly as ordained ministers ("The Freedom of a Christian" [1520], reprinted in *Martin Luther's Basic Theological Writings*, 2nd ed., ed. Timothy F. Lull [Augsburg Fortress, 2005], 398-400).

- Reread 1 Corinthians 3:5-15, replacing the names Apollos and Paul with your own names. As members of the priesthood of the baptized, what are you being called to do? What tasks do you or can you perform in God's field, in God's temple?

Notes

SESSION TWO

Notes

2. The Latin phrase *simul justus et peccator* sums up Martin Luther's view of the Christian as a person who is "simultaneously saint and sinner." This means that the baptized are like sick people who are in the care of a physician who is at work healing them. The baptized are saints in the hope and to the extent that healing is taking place.

- List the words and phrases Paul uses in 1 Corinthians 3:1-4 to convey the same idea as "simultaneously saint and sinner." How does Paul's language help us understand Luther's theological point? How does Luther's language help us understand Paul's point?
- Why do Christians, past and present, experience quarrels and divisions? How might Paul's advice in the rest of the session Scripture text help us to refocus on what is really important?

Devotional Context

1. Think about your journey of faith and the persons who have nurtured and nourished your faith. Identify and name the persons who laid the foundations of your faith, planted it, watered it, and so on.

2. Review the mission of your congregation. Identify, if you can, those who planted the congregation, the charter members, and those who built on the foundations that these people laid. Who is doing ministry in your congregation today? How many people are engaged in this ministry?

3. Reflect on your own daily life and your occupation, community involvement, and activities. Would you call any of this ministry? Why or why not? If you went through your daily routine mindful that you were exercising the priesthood of the baptized, how might that affect what you do and how you do it?

Wrap-up

Be ready to look back over the work your group has done in this session.

Pray

Gracious God, we thank you for raising up committed servants like Paul and Apollos, who planted and watered the faith of the first Christians. We thank you for all men and women through the ages who have been faithful stewards of the good news. We thank you especially for those men and women who have nurtured and nourished our faith. Empower us to be faithful servants and stewards of your gospel and your grace. In Jesus' name we pray. Amen.

Extending the Conversation

Homework

1. Read the next session's Bible text: 1 Corinthians 6:12-20 and 10:23-33.

2. In your prayers this week, thank God for the persons who were instrumental in nurturing your faith. If possible, call or write these persons and tell them what a difference they have made in your life.

3. Exercise your priesthood of the baptized by doing one or more of the following: praying for each other and anyone you feel is in special need; personally forgiving someone who has hurt or offended you (if you can't do this in person, consider writing a letter—it doesn't matter if they don't respond); offering to teach or help with Sunday school or another children's or youth ministry; becoming a mentor to a young person in your congregation; sharing your faith story with a child (in person or in writing); volunteering at a homeless shelter, food pantry, or other agency; visiting the sick or shut-in; helping to keep your community clean and safe; or becoming more aware of and/or engaged in local issues.

Enrichment

1. If you want to read all of 1 and 2 Corinthians during this unit, read the following sections this week.
- Day 1: 1 Corinthians 3:1-23
- Day 2: 1 Corinthians 4:1-20
- Day 3: 1 Corinthians 5:1—6:20
- Day 4: 1 Corinthians 7:1-39
- Day 5: 1 Corinthians 8:1-13
- Day 6: 1 Corinthians 9:1-27
- Day 7: 1 Corinthians 10:1—11:1

2. To understand current Lutheran thinking on the priesthood of the baptized, visit the Web site of the Evangelical Lutheran Church in America (www.elca.org). Click on "Growing in Faith," "Vocation," and then "Ministry in Daily Life." Explore the various articles on that page, especially those under "Ministry in Daily Life Theology."

3. Watch the movie *Babette's Feast* (Panorama Films A/S, 1988) or *Chocolat* (Miramax Films, 2000). How is the reality that humans are *simul justus et peccator* (simultaneously saints and sinners) depicted and played out in these films?

For Further Reading

Dave Daubert and Tana Kjos, with Kelly A. Fryer, *Reclaiming the "V" Word: Renewing Life at Its Vocational Core* (Augsburg Fortress, 2009).

Frank G. Honeycutt, *Sanctified Living: More Than Grace and Forgiveness* (Augsburg Fortress, 2008).

Uwe Siemon-Netto, "Work Is Our Mission," *Christianity Today*, November 2007, 30-32.

 Notes

SESSION THREE

1 Corinthians 6:12-20; 10:23-33

Focus Statement
Freedom in Christ is not permission for selfish indulgence. Freedom in Christ liberates us for service to the other.

Key Verse
So, whether you eat or drink, or whatever you do, do everything for the glory of God.   1 Corinthians 10:31

It's Not All about Me?

 **Focus Image**

© PeskyMonkey / iStockphoto

Gather

Check-in
Take this time to connect or reconnect with the others in your group. Be ready to share new thoughts or insights about your last session.

Pray
Almighty God, by our baptism into the death and resurrection of your Son, Jesus Christ, you turn us from the old life of sin. Grant that we who are reborn to new life in him may live in righteousness and holiness all our days, through your Son, Jesus Christ our Lord. Amen. (ELW, p. 86)

Focus Activity
Take a few minutes to look at the Focus Image. Where have you encountered self-centered attitudes or actions recently? How did this impact your life? How did you respond? Reflect on how your self-centered attitudes or actions have affected the people you live and work with, their responses, and the end result for your relationships.

SESSION THREE

Open Scripture

Read 1 Corinthians 6:12-20 and 10:23-33.

- What words or phrases caught your attention?

- Was there anything surprising or troubling?

- What questions do these texts raise for you?

 Notes

Join the Conversation

Literary Context

1. Both 1 Corinthians 6:12-20 and 10:23-33 begin the same way: Paul quotes slogans used by some of the Corinthian church members. Write down the slogans quoted in 6:12 and 10:23. What do you think the Corinthian Christians meant by these slogans? What behaviors could they have been trying to rationalize? (See 5:1-8; 6:12-20; 8:1-13; and 10:14-33.)

2. Now write down Paul's responses to these slogans (again in 6:12 and 10:23). Discuss whether Paul agrees or disagrees with the Corinthian Christians. What values does he appear to be lifting up? Who should benefit and not be dominated by anything (6:12-20)? Who should benefit and be built up by things that church members do (10:23-33)?

3. Identify the guiding principle for Christian behavior, according to Paul. (See 6:20 and 10:31.)

Historical Context

1. Some ancient Greek philosophies described the body as a prison or tomb to be overcome, disciplined, or ignored. Some elite church members were visiting prostitutes, justifying their behavior as bodily activity, like eating, that had no spiritual effects (6:13). Thinking they

SESSION THREE

 **Notes**

were already spiritual people (3:1) free from bodily concerns led them to *libertinism*, the idea that anything and everything was permissible for them.

- Reread 1 Corinthians 6:12-20. Discuss Paul's understanding of the relationship between body and spirit, how one affects the other, and to whom our bodies belong.

2. The majority of people in the ancient world believed that pollution, disease, and misfortune were caused by invisible spiritual forces called *daimons*. Certain rituals were thought to ward off these negative forces and gain the favor of protective spirits or gods. These rituals often included animal sacrifices. The meat from sacrifices was eaten by worshippers in temples, taken home for celebratory meals, and sold in the marketplace. Sacrifices were thus the source of almost all available meat, which was almost always eaten in the context of worship or family celebration. Elite members of the church were educated in Greco-Roman philosophical traditions, which taught that daimons were not real, and so ritual interaction with them was just social convention without any spiritual or moral implications.

- Reread 1 Corinthians 8:1-13; 10:14-22; and 10:23—11:1 and note which group Paul seems to agree with. Which group is being asked to modify its behavior? Why?

Lutheran Context

1. In his book *The Cost of Discipleship* (first published in German in 1937; Simon & Schuster, 1996), Dietrich Bonhoeffer describes cheap grace as "the justification of sin without the justification of the sinner." Cheap grace says that God loves us just as we are and so nothing needs to change in our lives. Cheap grace results in a secularized Christianity indistinguishable from the wider culture, in which discipleship is replaced by a program focusing on personal success and happiness.

- Compare the libertinism of elites in the Corinthian church with the concept of cheap grace. Now consider Paul's comment in 1 Corinthians 6:20. Is God's grace free? Who pays the price? What does Paul suggest as an appropriate response on our part?

- Think back to last session's discussion of the priesthood of the baptized. How is the idea of cheap grace at odds with our baptismal calling to the priesthood of the baptized?

2. First Corinthians 8–10 is part of the biblical basis for Lutheran theological reflection on the importance of "the bound conscience." Reread 1 Corinthians 8:7-13 and 10:23-30. What does Paul say here

about respecting the conscience of the other? Why is this important, according to Paul?

- Notice that God is at work in both kingdoms, in different ways. What are some other similarities or differences between the two kingdoms?

Devotional Context

1. Paul describes how visiting prostitutes negatively affects both the individual bodies of believers ("your bodies," 6:15-18) and the body of the church in which God's Spirit dwells ("your body," 6:19-20; see also 3:16). What physical activities have been, or perhaps still are, regarded as inappropriate or destructive for individual believers and for the church as a whole? What is the relationship between our behavior as individuals and our behavior as Christians?

2. In first-century Corinth eating meat that came from pagan sacrifices was a problem because it was such a widespread cultural practice that it was almost impossible to avoid. It raised questions about Christian identity. How far could a Christian go along with these practices and still be a Christian?

- Are there any similar issues in our contemporary cultural context? Consider the following possibilities: Is being a faithful disciple of Jesus Christ always compatible with fitting in comfortably with your peer group? Being a good employee? Being a good citizen?

Wrap-up

Be ready to look back over the work your group has done in this session.

Pray

Create in me a clean heart, O God, and put a new and right spirit within me. Keep me always mindful, Lord, that I am yours—body, mind, and soul; that your Spirit dwells in me and in the people around me. Help me remember that my behavior affects all those people for good or ill. May my words and my actions be instruments of your love and grace. In Jesus' name I pray. Amen.

Extending the Conversation

Homework

1. Read the next session's Bible text: 1 Corinthians 12:1-31.

2. Spend some time each day reflecting on the session title, "It's Not All about Me?" and/or the Focus Image. Write in a journal about

 Notes

SESSION THREE

 Notes

situations where it was or might be helpful for you to remember "It's not all about me." Paul claims that our words and actions affect others around us and reflect on our claim to be Christians. How does being mindful of this affect the way you behave?

3. How prevalent is "cheap grace" in contemporary Christian messages? Take time to scrutinize the content of Christian radio or television messages, the words and lyrics of your favorite hymns and Christian music, your usual devotional materials or other Christian books you are reading, and Christian Web sites. Consider reporting back to the group on what you find.

Enrichment

1. If you want to read all of 1 and 2 Corinthians during this unit, read the following sections this week.
- Day 1: 1 Corinthians 10:1-22
- Day 2: 1 Corinthians 10:23—11:1
- Day 3: 1 Corinthians 11:2-16
- Day 4: 1 Corinthians 11:17-22
- Day 5: 1 Corinthians 11:23-34
- Day 6: 1 Corinthians 12:1-11
- Day 7: 1 Corinthians 12:12-31

2. Learn more about Dietrich Bonhoeffer—the man, his life, and his theology—by viewing one of these films: *Bonhoeffer: Agent of Grace* (Vision Video, 2000) or *Bonhoeffer: Pastor, Pacifist, Nazi Resister* (First Run Features, 2003).

3. To learn more about the Lutheran concept of the "bound conscience," visit www.elca.org and read the following articles: "FAQs on Bound Conscience," "Remarks concerning 'Bound Conscience' Presented to the 2009 Churchwide Assembly by the Rev. Dr. Timothy J. Wengert," and "Reflections on the Bound Conscience in Lutheran Theology" by Timothy J. Wengert.

For Further Reading

Renate Bethge, *Dietrich Bonhoeffer: A Brief Life* (Fortress, 2004).

Dietrich Bonhoeffer, *The Cost of Discipleship* (first published in German in 1937; Simon & Schuster, 1996).

SESSION FOUR

1 Corinthians 12:1-31

Learner Session Guide

Focus Statement
The Holy Spirit gives each person a gift that is indispensable to the body of Christ.

Key Verse
On the contrary, the members of the body that seem to be weaker are indispensable, and those members of the body that we think less honorable we clothe with greater honor, and our less respectable members are treated with greater respect.
1 Corinthians 12:22-23

What Am I Good For?

 Focus Image

© Beata Beckla / iStockphoto

Gather

Check-in
Take this time to connect or reconnect with the others in your group. Be ready to share new thoughts or insights about your last session.

Pray
Almighty God, your Holy Spirit equips the church with a rich variety of gifts. Grant that we may use them to bear witness to Christ in lives that are built on faith and love. Make us ready to live the gospel and eager to do your will, so that we may share with all your church in the joys of eternal life; through Jesus Christ, our Savior and Lord. Amen. (ELW, p. 76)

Focus Activity
Take a few moments to examine the Focus Image. How does a finger, hand, eye, or toe contribute to the overall functioning and well-being of a human body? Reflecting on your membership in the church, what part of the body do you feel most like, and why?

SESSION FOUR

 **Notes**

Open Scripture

Read 1 Corinthians 12:1-31.

- What words or phrases caught your attention?

- What people or situations were called to mind?

- What issues or concerns does this text raise for you?

Join the Conversation

Historical Context

1. The topic in 1 Corinthians 12:1-11 is *pneumatika,* literally phenomena induced by the Spirit, but usually translated as "spiritual gifts." In the cultural environment of ancient Mediterranean societies, the existence of spirits, both good and bad, was taken for granted. The challenge was to discern what phenomena were genuinely induced by God's Holy Spirit.

- Look over 1 Corinthians 12:1-11. What criteria does Paul suggest for discerning who or what is truly inspired by the Spirit?

2. Greco-Roman political rhetoric frequently presented the body as a symbol of society in order to encourage social harmony. This political rhetoric insisted that a healthy body (society) was one in which every part was in its proper place and doing its assigned tasks. The head and its parts (mind, eyes, ears, and so on) had the highest status, providing direction and guidance for the rest of the body. The lowest-ranking parts (persons) were covered up, hidden from public view, and without public voice. The end goal of this rhetoric was to reinforce and maintain the distinctions that separated rulers from those they ruled over.

- Read 1 Corinthians 12:12-31 and compare Paul's idea of the church as the body of Christ to the Greco-Roman political rhetoric about society as a body. What aspects of the body does Paul emphasize?
- Imagine how the different members of Paul's congregation in Corinth would hear and respond to this teaching. Who was Paul trying to affirm and empower? Who was Paul trying to correct and change? Discuss whether this type of affirmation and correction is needed in the church today.

Literary Context

1. Paul says in the session Scripture text that through the Holy Spirit God activates or energizes three forms of *pneumatika*: *charismata*—gifts or graces given to the individual; *diakonia*—service-oriented ministries; and *energemata*—energizing or inspiring activities.

- List the spiritual gifts mentioned by Paul in 1 Corinthians 12:8-10 and 12:28. Which of these gifts would you identify as individual gifts or graces? Service-oriented ministries? Energizing or inspiring activities?
- Are all of the spiritual gifts that Paul mentions still active in the church today? Are some gifts more prevalent than others?

2. Some members of the church in Corinth were arguing that speaking in tongues was more important than other spiritual gifts. Paul's response to this argument is in 1 Corinthians 13 and 14.

- Read 1 Corinthians 13 and list the characteristics of love and of speaking in tongues and other spiritual gifts. What similarities and differences do you see? How does this connect with Paul's comments in 1 Corinthians 12:7 and 12:21-26?
- How might Paul's vision of love shape the way we think about being the body of Christ?

Lutheran Context

1. Martin Luther explains the work of the Holy Spirit in individuals, the church, and the world in his explanation of the Third Article of the Apostles' Creed ("I believe in the Holy Spirit . . ."):

> I believe that by my own understanding or strength I cannot believe in Jesus Christ my Lord or come to him, but instead the Holy Spirit has called me through the gospel, enlightened me with his gifts, made me holy, and kept me in the true faith, just as he calls, gathers, enlightens, and makes holy the whole Christian church on earth and keeps it with Jesus Christ in the one common, true faith. (*Luther's Small Catechism with* Evangelical Lutheran Worship *Texts* [Augsburg Fortress, 2008], 16)

SESSION FOUR

 **Notes**

- What words and phrases in this statement help us better understand what Paul is trying to get at in 1 Corinthians 12:1-11? How does Paul's message help us understand Luther's point in the Small Catechism?

2. Using the Lutheran principle of "Scripture interprets Scripture," we read passages from other parts of the Bible to shed light on the meaning of a text.

- Read Leviticus 19:33-34; Isaiah 56:1-8; Matthew 20:24-28; and John 13:1-17. What is the main point or lesson in each of these texts? How do these texts help us understand Paul's teaching in 1 Corinthians 12:12-26? How does Paul's message help us understand these other passages?

3. Lutherans read Scripture through the lenses of law and gospel. Law judges and convicts us and challenges us to change our ways. Gospel causes God's grace and love to reach out to us, comforting and sustaining us. Law and gospel are present throughout the Bible.

- When you read 1 Corinthians 12:12-26, where do you hear law? Where do you hear gospel?

Devotional Context

1. The focus statement for this session is "The Holy Spirit gives each person a gift that is indispensable to the body of Christ." Go around the room and name a gift or blessing that each person contributes to the group. You might use the following format:

> [*Name*], you are good for [*gift or blessing*].

2. The Holy Spirit is given to us in the sacrament of Holy Baptism. Reflect on how the Holy Spirit has been and is still active in your life. Share your thoughts with the group.

Wrap-up

Be ready to look back over the work your group has done in this session.

Pray

We give you thanks, O God, that through water and the Holy Spirit you give us new birth, cleanse us from sin, and raise us to eternal life. Stir up in your people the gift of your Holy Spirit: the spirit of wisdom and understanding, the spirit of counsel and might, the spirit of knowledge and the fear of the Lord, the spirit of joy in your presence, both now and forever. Amen. (ELW, p. 237)

SESSION FOUR

Extending the Conversation

Homework

1. Read the next session's Bible text: 1 Corinthians 15:12-28, 35-58.

2. To discover your own spiritual gifts, complete the spiritual gifts assessment available at www.elca.org/Growing-in-Faith/Ministry/Women-of-the-ELCA/All-Our-Resources/Affirming-Our-Gifts/Spiritual-Gifts-Discovery.aspx. Once you have completed the assessment, reflect on how you use your gifts to build up the body of Christ. Perhaps it's time to become more involved in some way!

3. Look around your congregation and/or community. Who feels weak, dispensable, less honorable, or less respectable? Why do they feel that way? Are there things you could do to change that? What can you do to show these people that they are honored and respected and appreciated for their presence? Make a plan and act on it. Get others involved too.

Enrichment

1. If you want to read all of 1 and 2 Corinthians during this unit, read the following sections this week.
- Day 1: 1 Corinthians 13:1-13
- Day 2: 1 Corinthians 14:1-25
- Day 3: 1 Corinthians 14:26-40
- Day 4: 1 Corinthians 15:1-11
- Day 5: 1 Corinthians 15:12-34
- Day 6: 1 Corinthians 15:35-58
- Day 7: 1 Corinthians 16:1-24

2. Read the ABC News *Nightline* story "Speaking in Tongues: Alternative Voices in Faith" at http://abcnews.go.com/Nightline/story?id=2935819&page=1. Reflect on your reactions and thoughts about speaking in tongues.

For Further Reading

Yung Suk Kim, *Christ's Body in Corinth: The Politics of a Metaphor* (Fortress Press, 2008).

Lois Malcolm, *Holy Spirit: Creative Power in Our Lives* (Augsburg Fortress, 2009).

Dale B. Martin, *The Corinthian Body* (Yale University Press, 1999).

Notes

SESSION FIVE

1 Corinthians 15:12-28, 35-58

Learner Session Guide

 Focus Statement

In the resurrection we will be like Christ and with Christ in God, who will be all in all.

 Key Verse

Just as we have borne the image of the man of dust, we will also bear the image of the man of heaven.
1 Corinthians 15:49

What Will I Be Ultimately?

 Focus Image

© Nadya Lukio / iStockphoto

Gather

Check-in

Take this time to connect or reconnect with the others in your group. Be ready to share new thoughts or insights about your last session.

Pray

God of mercy, we no longer look for Jesus among the dead, for he is alive and has become the Lord of life. Increase in our minds and hearts the risen life we share with Christ, and help us to grow as your people toward the fullness of eternal life with you, through Jesus Christ, our Savior and Lord, who lives and reigns with you and the Holy Spirit, one God, now and forever. Amen. (ELW, p. 32)

Focus Activity

How would you answer the question, "What will I be ultimately?" Draw, sketch, or doodle a picture, image, or symbol representing your understanding of your final destiny.

SESSION FIVE

Open Scripture

Read 1 Corinthians 15:12-28, 35-58.

- What words or phrases caught your attention?

- What images, sounds, or situations do these texts call to mind?

- What questions do these passages raise for you?

 Notes

Join the Conversation

Historical Context

1. Ancient peoples had differing opinions about the "end" or final destiny of individual persons, entire societies, and the world itself. Greco-Roman beliefs focused on individuals—what happens to people when they die. While some Greeks and Romans insisted that this life is all there is, most believed the souls of the dead went to nasty or nice regions of Hades, depending on what they deserved. Many people were initiated into various mystery religions, hoping that at death their souls would be freed from imprisonment in physical bodies and join the gods in the starry heavens.

- Compare Greco-Roman beliefs about the end with the session Scripture text. What similarities and differences do you see?

2. Israelites imagined the souls of the dead residing in an underworld called Sheol. By the first century, many believed the souls of the righteous were gathered into a heavenly place (such as Abraham's bosom). Some within Judaism insisted that our final destiny lay beyond the afterlife: resurrection of the body into a new life in a new world and a new age established by God. The focus of Israelite beliefs about the end, however, was not only on what happens to individuals

SESSION FIVE

 Notes

when they die, but on God's ultimate plan for all of creation—what happens to the heavens and the earth and all they contain.

- What is Paul trying to explain in 1 Corinthians 15:12-28 and 15:35-58? How does this text compare with Jewish beliefs about the end? What does Paul focus on?

Literary Context

1. Major themes in Christian beliefs about the end are derived from the session Scripture text and other New Testament passages. In 1 Corinthians 15, Paul writes about the ultimate goal of Christ's mission, and key events in the unfolding of that mission.

- Read 1 Corinthians 15:20-28 closely. Identify what Paul understands to be the ultimate goal of Christ's mission in human history, and four key events that take place as that mission unfolds. Are these past, present, or future events?

- Identify what the following texts say about the end, and discuss whether all of these are equally important for understanding the goals and purposes of Christ's mission as we participate in it here and now.

Romans 8:18-24	Matthew 13:24-30
1 Thessalonians 4:13-18	Revelation 20:1-15

2. To drive home what he is saying, Paul contrasts "pre-resurrection bodies" with "post-resurrection bodies." List the characteristics of each type of body, as described in 1 Corinthians 15:35-58. How are these bodies similar? How are they different?

3. It is often difficult to translate terms precisely from one language to another. Consider this: In 1 Corinthians 15:44 Paul distinguishes between two different kinds of bodies using the Greek phrases *soma psychikon* versus *soma pneumatikon*. While *pneumatikon* does mean "spiritual," *psychikon* derives from the Greek word *psyche*, often translated as "soul" or "life principle." Greek-speaking Jews like Paul often used *psyche* to refer to "mind." It is the root of our English term *psychology*, the study of mental functions and behaviors.

- Discuss what it might mean that in the resurrection *psyche* will be transformed into *pneuma*. What is the distinction that Paul is trying to draw? How does this compare with what you believe about the end?

Lutheran Context

1. The Lutheran reformers accepted the Nicene Creed and the Apostles' Creed as true statements of the Christian faith. Lutherans today continue to accept these creeds and use them in worship.

- Read the words of the Nicene Creed and the Apostles' Creed (ELW, pp. 104–105). What is the primary focus of these creeds—the ultimate destiny of individual persons or of all creation? What words and phrases support your conclusions?

2. In the Formula of Concord the Lutheran reformers write, "Concerning the article on the resurrection Scripture testifies that this very substance of our flesh, albeit without sin, will rise, and that we will have and retain this soul, albeit without sin, in eternal life" (*The Book of Concord: The Confessions of the Evangelical Lutheran Church*, ed. Robert Kolb and Timothy J. Wengert [Fortress Press, 2000], 539.46). What they are saying is that the whole person (body, mind, soul) will be resurrected into eternal life, but without sin and its effects.

- How does this Lutheran theological insight help us to see what the difference is between pre-resurrection and post-resurrection bodies (1 Corinthians 15:35-58)? How does Paul's description of post-resurrection bodies help us better understand how sin affects human beings?

Devotional Context

1. Spend a few moments just looking at the Focus Image, then discuss the following questions:

- As an illustration of life in the resurrection, what does this photograph suggest about what it means to be like Christ? What does it imply about being with Christ in God? What does it say about where God is and will be?

- How does this image compare with the one you drew at the beginning of this session? Looking back on that picture now, would you change anything? Why or why not?

2. Write down your responses to these questions:

- How is the session Scripture text good news for you personally? How does the promise that you will one day bear the image of "the man of heaven" (1 Corinthians 15:49) affect the way you live your life on a daily basis?

- What difference does Christ's resurrection make in how you view the world in which you live? How does Paul's statement that the end goal of Christ's mission is that God will be all in all (1 Corinthians 15:28) affect your personal vocation and/or the mission of your congregation?

Wrap-up

Be ready to look back over the work your group has done in this session.

Notes

SESSION FIVE

 Notes

Pray

Lord of Life, whom death could not hold, we praise and adore you. Your resurrection was unexpected, amazing, and almost unbelievable, but now we know that the grave is not our final destiny. Now we can be sure that nothing is hopeless. Broken relationships . . . sickness . . . distress of any kind . . . conflict . . . and even death . . . will not have the final word. Because you live we can live life to the fullest, knowing that we have everything to live for today, tomorrow, and forever. Amen.

Extending the Conversation

Homework

1. Read the next session's Bible text: 2 Corinthians 3:1—4:15.

2. Spend some time each day reflecting on what you have learned in this session. How is each day of your life a step toward that final destiny? This might be an opportunity for some soul-searching. Is God "all" in your life? What stands in the way of God becoming "all"? If God were "all," how would your daily life be different?

3. Begin each day by reading 1 Corinthians 15:58. Make it the goal of your day to be steadfast in doing the Lord's work in all the situations and places where you find yourself. Take time to identify situations and places—big and small—where you see God at work or where the gospel is needed, and consider how you might be part of that work.

Enrichment

1. If you want to read all of 1 and 2 Corinthians during this unit, read the following sections this week.
- Day 1: 1 Corinthians 15:35-58
- Day 2: 1 Corinthians 16:1-24
- Day 3: 2 Corinthians 1:1-11
- Day 4: 2 Corinthians 1:12—2:4
- Day 5: 2 Corinthians 2:5-17
- Day 6: 2 Corinthians 3:1-18
- Day 7: 2 Corinthians 4:1-15

2. Part 3 of Handel's sacred oratorio *Messiah* is based on selected verses from 1 Corinthians 15. Listen to a recording or performance of this music. How does Handel's musical interpretation affect your understanding of Paul's message?

3. Make time to view the film *What Dreams May Come* (1998), starring Robin Williams and Cuba Gooding Jr. How are the beliefs about final destiny depicted in the film similar to and/or different from biblical understandings of what Christ does for us?

SESSION FIVE

For Further Reading

Alister E. McGrath, *Resurrection* (Fortress Press, 2007).

Barbara R. Rossing, *The Rapture Exposed: The Message of Hope in the Book of Revelation* (Basic Books, 2004).

Robert B. Stewart, ed., *The Resurrection of Jesus: John Dominic Crossan and N. T. Wright in Dialogue* (Fortress Press, 2005).

SESSION SIX

2 Corinthians 3:1—4:15

Learner Session Guide

 Focus Statement

Our transformation into the image of Christ is entirely the work of the Holy Spirit.

 Key Verse

And all of us, with unveiled faces, seeing the glory of the Lord as though reflected in a mirror, are being transformed into the same image from one degree of glory to another; for this comes from the Lord, the Spirit.
2 Corinthians 3:18

How Do I Achieve This Glory?

 Focus Image

FreeWine (Flickr). Used by Creative Commons 2.0 Attribution License.

Gather

Check-in

Take this time to connect or reconnect with the others in your group. Be ready to share new thoughts or insights about your last session.

Pray

Holy God, mighty and immortal, you are beyond our knowing, yet we see your glory in the face of Jesus Christ. Transform us into the likeness of your Son, who renewed our humanity so that we may share in his divinity, Jesus Christ our Lord, who lives and reigns with you and the Holy Spirit, one God, now and forever. Amen. (ELW, p. 26)

Focus Activity

Spend a few minutes contemplating the Focus Image. If the sun's reflection in the water was your only source of information about the sun, what would you know about the sun, and what information might you miss? If the sun's reflection on the paddle was your only source of information about the sun, what would you know about the sun, and what information might you miss? Is our perception of God more like looking at the sun, looking at reflections of the sun in the water, or looking at reflections of sun and water on the paddle?

SESSION SIX

Open Scripture

Read 2 Corinthians 3:1—4:15.

 Notes

- What words, phrases, or images caught your attention?

- What questions does this passage raise?

- What is the tone of this passage? How does it make you feel?

Historical Context

1. People of Jewish faith observed the Law or Torah (Genesis, Exodus, Leviticus, Numbers, and Deuteronomy). While most early followers of Jesus were people of Jewish faith, this began to change as the gospel message spread to non-Jews (Gentiles). By the middle of the first century, the controversy that dominated the church, and Paul's ministry as well, involved admitting non-Jews into the church. This controversy reached the Corinthian congregation in the form of Jewish Christian apostles (2 Corinthians 11:22), who brought letters of recommendation (3:1) and visited the church in Paul's absence. These apostles insisted that Gentile believers abide by the Torah in order to be saved. This message was creating doubt and confusion among church members in Corinth.

- How would you imagine Gentile believers reacted to this message?

2. Paul heard about the activities of the Jewish Christian apostles and the confusion they were creating in the church. Today's text is part of his response.

- As 2 Corinthians 3:1-16 is read, list characteristics of the "new covenant" and "old covenant."
- Review the contrasts between the new and old covenants. What seems to be Paul's point? How is his message relevant in our own times?

SESSION SIX

 Notes

Literary Context

1. Both sides of the debate over accepting Gentiles into the church appealed to the Hebrew Scriptures. In the session Scripture text, Paul draws upon Exodus 34 to make his case. In the story from Exodus, God tells Moses to bring two stone tablets to the top of Mount Sinai. There God gives the Ten Commandments and tells Moses to write the words on the stone tablets. When Moses comes down from the mountain with the commandments, his face reflects God's glory. Moses wears a veil over his face when he is among the people, but he removes the veil whenever he speaks with God.

- Read through 2 Corinthians 3:7—4:6. Fill in the rest of the chart below and discuss how Paul uses the text from Exodus to make his case. According to Paul, who or what is covered by a veil, and why? How is the veil removed?

Old covenant	New covenant
Stone tablets (2 Corinthians 3:3, 7; Exodus 34:1, 4)	Tablets of human hearts (2 Corinthians 3:3)
Old covenant of letters (2 Corinthians 3:14; Exodus 34:10-28)	(2 Corinthians 3:6)
Encountering God results in Moses' shining face (2 Corinthians 3:7; Exodus 34:29-30)	(2 Corinthians 3:8-11, 18)
The veil over Moses' face (2 Corinthians 3:13; Exodus 34:33)	(2 Corinthians 3:14-15)
Moses takes off the veil before the Lord (2 Corinthians 3:16; Exodus 34:34)	(2 Corinthians 3:14, 16)

2. Paul emphasizes that salvation is entirely the Holy Spirit's work by using images that contrast human fragility with the gospel's power. God enlightens and empowers us to overcome life's afflictions and in doing so joins us to the death and resurrected life of Jesus.

- Read 2 Corinthians 4:6-15. Underline images of human fragility and circle images of the gospel's power.

- In 2 Corinthians 4:11-12 Paul asserts that we carry in our bodies simultaneously the death and life of Jesus. How might this be part of the process of transforming us into the image of Christ (2 Corinthians 3:18)?

Lutheran Context

1. Martin Luther writes about the work of the Holy Spirit:

> I believe that by my own understanding or strength I cannot believe in Jesus Christ my Lord or come to him, but instead the Holy Spirit has called me through the gospel, enlightened me with his gifts, made me holy, and kept me in the true faith, just as he calls, gathers, enlightens, and makes holy the whole Christian church on earth and

34   1, 2 Corinthians Learner Guide

keeps it with Jesus Christ in the one common, true faith. (explanation of the Third Article of the Apostles' Creed, *Luther's Small Catechism with* Evangelical Lutheran *Worship Texts* [Augsburg Fortress, 2008], 16)

- How do Luther's words help us understand Paul's message in the session Scripture text? Think of the different ways you hear people in church, in the media, and in society describe faith and the process of salvation. How is Paul's message relevant today?

2. Paul states that "the letter kills, but the Spirit gives life" (2 Corinthians 3:6). Martin Luther connects this to two kinds of preaching: law and gospel. He writes, "[I]t is impossible for someone who does not first hear the law and let himself be killed by the letter, to hear the gospel and let the grace of the Spirit bring him to life. . . . No one can have the one without the other" ("Concerning the Letter and the Spirit," in *Martin Luther's Basic Theological Writings*, 2nd ed., ed. Timothy F. Lull [Augsburg Fortress, 2005], 83). The law demands, accuses, and judges, in order to open us up to the promise, comfort, and grace of the gospel.

- Review 2 Corinthians 3:1—4:15. Where do you hear law? Where do you hear gospel?

Devotional Context

1. Reflect back on the Focus Image. Jot down, doodle, or draw your responses to the following questions:

- Where do you encounter the glory of the Lord? How?
- How do you see God reflected in others?
- How might others see God reflected in you?

2. Our ultimate destiny is to be like Christ and with Christ in God, who will be all in all. Today's session asks the question, "How do I achieve this glory?"

- Name some ways that the session Scripture text affirms, surprises, or disturbs you and your understanding of salvation.
- In your own words, summarize how 2 Corinthians 3:1—4:15 helps you understand how we become more like Christ. Who does all the work and who should get all the credit? How is the "old covenant" of the letter or the law helpful in this process?
- Give one example of how the Holy Spirit has been transforming you in your journey of faith.

Wrap-up

Be ready to look back over the work your group has done in this session.

Notes

SESSION SIX

 **Notes**

Pray

Come, Holy Spirit! Come into my life, be with me, and help me to see God more clearly in the world and in the people around me. Come, Holy Spirit! Come into my life, cleanse my heart, and help me to let go of those things—sins, opinions, habits, prejudices, possessions, or whatever they are—that keep me from loving you. Come, Holy Spirit! Come into my life, change me, mold me, and make me more and more like Jesus. Amen.

Extending the Conversation

Homework

1. Read the next session's Bible text: 2 Corinthians 4:16—5:21.

2. Read Paul's description of the works of the flesh and the fruits of the Spirit in Galatians 5:16-26, and consider what the Holy Spirit is doing in your life. How can you open up more time and space in your life for the Holy Spirit's transformative work?

3. Organize a prayer group committed to helping each other develop the practice of daily prayer. Seek advice from your pastor or other spiritual leader or use a book like Martha Grace Reese's *Unbinding Your Heart: 40 Days of Prayer and Faith Sharing* (Chalice Press, 2008) to get started. Helpful resources are also available online:

- ELCA Prayer Center: www.elca.org/What-We-Believe/Prayer-Center.aspx
- Centering Prayer: www.centeringprayer.com
- Fixed-Hour Prayer: www.phyllistickle.com/fixedhourprayer.html
- "Centered by Prayer" article by Kimberly Winston: http://faithandleadership.duke.edu/features/articles/centered-prayer

Enrichment

1. If you want to read all of 1 and 2 Corinthians during this unit, read the following sections this week.

- Day 1: 2 Corinthians 3:1-18
- Day 2: 2 Corinthians 4:1-15
- Day 3: 2 Corinthians 4:16—5:10
- Day 4: 2 Corinthians 5:11-21
- Day 5: 2 Corinthians 6:1-13
- Day 6: 2 Corinthians 6:14—7:1
- Day 7: 2 Corinthians 7:2-16

SESSION SIX

2. Check out the following Web site for ideas about how to deepen your faith and spirituality: http://www.elca.org/Growing-in-Faith/Vocation/Rostered-Leadership/Leadership-Support/Health/Wholeness-Wheel.aspx. Read the quote from Martin Luther at the top of the page. Consider how this quote connects with 2 Corinthians 3:1—4:15. What does the Wholeness Wheel suggest about how the Holy Spirit is active in our lives?

3. Visit http://www.practicingourfaith.org/what-are-christian-practices and read about Christian practices that draw us into God's activity in the world and reflect God's grace and love.

For Further Reading

Dorothy C. Bass, *Practicing Our Faith: A Way of Life for a Searching People*, 2nd ed. (Jossey-Bass, 2010).

Robert Benson, *In Constant Prayer* (Thomas Nelson, 2008).

Lois Malcolm, *Holy Spirit: Creative Power in Our Lives* (Augsburg Fortress, 2009).

Notes

SESSION SEVEN

2 Corinthians
4:16—5:21

Learner Session Guide

 Focus Statement

In Christ we are invited to participate in God's mission of reconciliation.

 Key Verse

So we are ambassadors for Christ, since God is making his appeal through us; we entreat you on behalf of Christ, be reconciled to God.
2 Corinthians 5:20

What Can I Do Here and Now?

 Focus Image

© thumb / iStockphoto

Gather

Check-in

Take this time to connect or reconnect with the others in your group. Be ready to share new thoughts or insights about your last session.

Pray

Grant, O God, that your holy and life-giving Spirit may move every human heart; that the barriers which divide us may crumble, suspicions disappear, and hatreds cease; and that, with our divisions healed, we might live in justice and peace; through your Son, Jesus Christ our Lord. Amen. (*Evangelical Lutheran Worship, Pastoral Care* [Augsburg Fortress, 2008], 381)

Focus Activity

Take a few moments to contemplate the message in the Focus Image. Journal your responses to the following questions:

- How does this message speak to you personally?
- Is this a message directed at you? If so, who is calling you to come back? Why?
- Is this a message you want to send to someone else? Why?

SESSION SEVEN

Open Scripture

Read 2 Corinthians 4:16—5:21.

- What words, phrases, or images touched you?

- How does this passage make you feel?

- What questions does this passage raise for you?

Notes

Join the Coversation

Historical Context

1. In the session Scripture text, Paul continues to explain the nature of the new covenant, which consists of the experience and work of the Holy Spirit in the lives of believers, not obedience to the laws of Moses. The Spirit works to transform all (both Jewish and Gentile believers) into the image of Christ (2 Corinthians 3:18).

- Read 2 Corinthians 4:7—5:5 and note what the Holy Spirit guarantees and how the Spirit is active in the lives of believers. Is this how you experience the Holy Spirit in your life and in your journey of faith?

2. As mentioned in session 5, ancient Greeks and Romans believed that the soul escapes from the prison of the physical body when a person dies.

- Reread 2 Corinthians 4:16—5:9, paying close attention to Paul's language and metaphors. What point is Paul trying to make here about our ultimate destiny? Discuss how Paul's point of view compares or contrasts with ancient Greco-Roman beliefs.

Literary Context

1. Studying key words and phrases in a Scripture text can help us better understand the writer's message. In 2 Corinthians 4:16—5:21 Paul uses two sets of terms: *reconciliation, renewed,* and *new creation*; and *judgment, recompense,* and *fear of the Lord*. *Reconciliation* is commonly defined as the reestablishment of friendly relations; in theology it

SESSION SEVEN

 **Notes**

refers to ending the separation between God and humans caused by sin. *Renewed* and *new creation*, as Paul uses them here, suggest that God's goal is not to restore things to the way they were, but to create an entirely new set of relationships. *Judgment* involves evaluating evidence in light of particular values or desired outcomes. *Recompense* means reward or punishment ("getting our just desserts"). *Fear of the Lord* refers to a sense of wonder and awe in God's presence.

- Identify which words and phrases relate to the goal of God's mission in the world, and which ones point to how that goal will be accomplished. How do these two sets of words and ideas relate to one another? How do they come together in Paul's description of the new covenant?

2. Another key term in the session Scripture text is *ambassador*. In the world of politics and diplomacy, an ambassador is an official messenger or representative for a country. Ambassadors are expected to be faithful to the country they represent, to not become entangled with customs where they are sent, and to return to their homeland at the appointed time.

- Look up the word *ambassador* in a dictionary and reflect on what it means to be "ambassadors for Christ" (2 Corinthians 5:20). How does this fit with the ministry of reconciliation?

Lutheran Context

1. Martin Luther's concept of the "happy exchange" explains how God reconciles us to God's self through Christ. It works like this: Christ has taken upon himself everything that belongs to us and has given to us everything that belongs to him. Consequently our sins are not reckoned to us but to Christ, and Christ gives his righteousness to us. In this life we remain sinners, but for Christ's sake God relates to us now as saints—at least saints in the making.

- If this is true, what is the purpose of God judging us according to the good and evil we have done while in the body (2 Corinthians 5:10)? What does judgment reveal about us and about God's grace?

2. Lutherans use the lenses of law and gospel to better understand Scripture. The law demands, accuses, and judges in order to open us up to the promise, comfort, and grace of the gospel. With your eyes closed, listen as someone reads aloud 2 Corinthians 4:16—5:21. What words of law and words of gospel do you hear? What does this suggest, if anything, about the condition of your relationship with God right now?

Devotional Context

1. Reconciliation is "a process of letting go of the past in order to live at peace in the future," according to William J. Danaher ("Some Reflections

on the Theology of Reconciliation," http://www.elca.org/What-We-Believe/Social-Issues/Journal-of-Lutheran-Ethics/Issues/March-2004/Some-Reflections-on-the-Theology-of-Reconciliation.aspx).

- Discuss how this definition of reconciliation might help us better understand what God is doing by reconciling us and the world to God's self through Christ, what the ministry of reconciliation that has been entrusted to us is about, and what we need to do in order to be reconciled with God and with one another.

2. Take another look at the Focus Image and at what you wrote down during the Focus Activity. Discuss how the words "come back" are related to the ministry of reconciliation God is engaged in and which has been entrusted to us. What are some common obstacles to reconciliation?

Wrap-up

Be ready to look back over the work your group has done in this session.

Pray

Gracious God, help me trust in your steadfast love. Draw me back to you when I lose my way. Give me the courage to reach out to those I have hurt, and the grace to forgive those who have hurt me. Empower me to be an ambassador of Christ and a minister of reconciliation in my family, my workplace, my neighborhood, and my church, so that no one is left out of your embrace. In Jesus' name I pray. Amen.

Extending the Conversation

Homework

1. Read the next session's Bible text: 2 Corinthians 8:1-15; 9:1-15.

2. Commit to seeking reconciliation with one person. Before contacting that person, spend some time reflecting on what happened in the past and what needs to be said or done (and by whom) in order to let go of the past so that you can have a relationship in the future. You may find it helpful to write all this down in a journal. Pray about it and ask for God's help. Then reach out to the person through a phone call, note, or e-mail inviting him or her to meet. Be clear about your reasons, hopes, and expectations for meeting. If the person agrees to a conversation, remember to listen as well as speak!

3. Consider organizing a small group to study and learn how to discuss difficult issues in your congregation. The following resources are available at http://www.elca.org/What-We-Believe/Social-Issues/Moral-Deliberation.aspx: "Talking Together as Christians

SESSION SEVEN

 **Notes**

about Tough Social Issues" and "Talking Together as Christians Cross Culturally: A Field Guide." Once your small group gains some confidence in doing this, ask each member to start and lead another small group.

Enrichment

1. If you want to read all of 1 and 2 Corinthians during this unit, read the following sections this week.

- Day 1: 2 Corinthians 8:1-15
- Day 2: 2 Corinthians 8:16—9:5
- Day 3: 2 Corinthians 9:6-15
- Day 4: 2 Corinthians 10:1-16
- Day 5: 2 Corinthians 10:17—11:15
- Day 6: 2 Corinthians 11:16—12:13
- Day 7: 2 Corinthians 12:14—13:10

2. Truth and reconciliation commissions have become a popular response to serious division and conflict in many countries. Search the Internet, beginning with Wikipedia, for articles on these commissions and the issues they have confronted. For an assessment of their success, view the documentary *Confronting the Truth: Truth Commissions and Societies in Transition* by Steve York and Neil J. Kritz (2007), available through the United States Institute for Peace Press (http://bookstore.usip.org).

3. Arrange for your group (along with others in your congregation) to view the movie *The Power of Forgiveness* (Journey Films, 2008). Discuss the role of forgiveness in processes of reconciliation. How does this connect with Paul's comments in 2 Corinthians 5:18-20?

For Further Reading

Kenneth Briggs, *The Power of Forgiveness* (Fortress Press, 2008).

Donald B. Kraybill, Steven M. Nolt, and David L. Weaver-Zercher, *Amish Grace: How Forgiveness Transcended Tragedy* (Jossey-Bass, 2010).

SESSION EIGHT

2 Corinthians
8:1-15; 9:1-15

Learner Session Guide

Focus Statement

God's grace produces blessings. Our response is gratitude in the form of thanksgiving to God and generosity toward those in need.

Key Verse

And God is able to provide you with every blessing in abundance, so that by always having enough of everything, you may share abundantly in every good work.
2 Corinthians 9:8

What Is My Response to God's Grace?

 Focus Image

© Kirby Hamilton / iStockphoto

Gather

Check-in

Take this time to connect or reconnect with the others in your group. Be ready to share new thoughts or insights about the last session.

Pray

Gracious God, you have given us so much. Teach us to appreciate your blessings and gifts. Help us to give generously and freely of all that you have given us. In Jesus' name we pray. Amen.

Focus Activity

Take a moment to reflect on the Focus Image. Name a wonderful gift you received from someone. How did you respond to this gift?

SESSION EIGHT

 Notes

Open Scripture

Read 2 Corinthians 8:1-15 9:1-15.

- What words, phrases, or images caught your attention?

- What is the main topic or issue that Paul is addressing?

- What is your first response to this teaching?

Historical Context

1. Aside from providing services to pilgrims visiting the temple for religious festivals, the city of Jerusalem had no significant industry or commercial base in biblical times. The temple derived revenue from tithes, offerings, and an annual tax collected by synagogues outside Judea. It is unlikely, however, that followers of Jesus in Jerusalem derived much, if any, economic benefit from the temple's activities. In the session Scripture texts, Paul encourages "the ministry to the saints"—a collection of funds for the support and relief of the church in Jerusalem.

- Read Paul's comments about this ministry in Galatians 2:1-10 and Romans 15:22-29. What other purposes might have been served by Paul's collection of funds for the Jerusalem church? What might the giving and receiving of this gift have symbolized?

2. Read 1 Corinthians 16:1-4 and 2 Corinthians 8:1-7. What do Paul's instructions suggest about the economic status of church members in the city of Corinth and in the Roman province of Macedonia? Are they much better off than church members in Jerusalem?

Literary Context

1. Many scholars regard 2 Corinthians as a compilation of fragments of letters that Paul wrote to the church over a period of a

year or more. The session Scripture texts are two such fragments written at different times. They remind church members of their commitment to the collection for the saints in Jerusalem (1 Corinthians 16:1-4).

- Reread 2 Corinthians 8:1-9 and 9:1-7. How does Paul go about encouraging the members of the church to participate in the collection? What strategies does he use? Discuss whether you would find Paul's appeal persuasive.

2. Paul uses the Greek word *charis* and related terms repeatedly in the session texts. The New Revised Standard Version of the Bible translates this in various ways.

Passage in 2 Corinthians	NRSV translation of *charis* and related terms
8:1; 9:14	"grace"
8:4	"privilege"
8:6-7, 19	"generous undertaking"
8:9	"generous act"
8:16; 9:15	"thanks"
9:8	"blessing"
9:11-12	"thanksgiving"

- Carefully reread the verses listed above. In each case, who is giving the charis, and who is receiving it? How are all these different uses of the word *grace* related to one another? Summarize the point you think Paul is trying to make in repeating charis and related words.

Lutheran Context

1. Martin Luther's emphasis on grace was the keystone of the Reformation, drawn from biblical texts such as Ephesians 2:8, "For by grace you have been saved through faith, and this is not your own doing; it is the gift of God." Luther insisted that grace is present at the beginning of faith, and is God's continuing action upon us. Grace comes to us "once for all, again and again, and more and more" (Monica Jyotsna Melanchthon, "The Grace of God and the Equality of Human Persons," *Dialog* [2003] 42, no. 1: 11).

- Read Luke 19:1-10. How do the actions of Zacchaeus relate to Luther's point about grace? How might Zacchaeus help us understand the point that Paul is making in 2 Corinthians 8:1-15 and 9:1-15?

SESSION EIGHT

 **Notes**

2. Using the principle of "Scripture interprets Scripture," Lutherans look at other portions of Scripture to help interpret a particular text.

- Read Philippians 2:6-11 and Romans 5:6-11. How do these texts deepen your understanding of Paul's message in 2 Corinthians 8?
- Discuss Paul's claim that Christ's incarnation and cross are the basis of Christian generosity toward those in need. Restate this claim in a way that emphasizes grace.

Devotional Context

1. Spend a few moments reflecting on your life and experience in light of 2 Corinthians 9:8. Journal your responses to the following questions:

- What blessings have you received from God?
- What do you have that did not come from God either directly or through others?
- Why do you think God has blessed you with these things?
- What have you done with the blessings that God has bestowed upon you?
- What should you be doing with the blessings you have received?

2. Brainstorm a list of current local, national, or global needs. Commit to one need as a group. Take up a collection, beginning right now if possible. Make arrangements to involve others in this collection. Set a deadline for the completion of the collection. Spend some time preparing a flyer, a temple talk, or another communication media that you can share with others.

Wrap-up

Be ready to look back over the work your group has done in this session.

Pray

God of abundance, you have poured out a large measure of earthly blessings: our table is richly furnished, our cup overflows, and we live in safety and security. Teach us to set our hearts on you and not these material blessings. Keep us from becoming captivated by prosperity, and grant us wisdom to use your blessings to your glory and to the service of humankind; through Jesus Christ our Lord. Amen. (ELW, p. 80)

Extending the Conversation

Homework

1. Each day during the coming week, meditate on 2 Corinthians 9:8. In your journal, write down how God has blessed you that day.

2. Commit yourself to the practice of gratitude and thanksgiving. Take some time each day to contact one person who has been a blessing to you.

3. Luther's explanation of the eighth commandment calls us to practice generosity of speech. Commit yourself to this spiritual discipline for the next week, and ask God to give you a generous spirit.

Enrichment

1. Watch the movie *Pay It Forward* (Warner Brothers, 2000), reflecting how good works done without expectation of a payback (in other words, grace) can change people's lives for the better.

2. Get involved in your congregation's stewardship ministry. Visit the Web site http://www2.elca.org/stewardship/makeitsimple for ideas about stewardship education and events for all ages.

3. If you are more of a history buff, enjoy a recap of Paul's ministry by viewing *Peter and Paul and the Christian Revolution*, available at www.pbs.org/peterandpaul.

For Further Reading

Bradley Hanson, *A Graceful Life: Lutheran Spirituality for Today* (Augsburg Fortress, 2000).

Mark Allan Powell, *Giving to God: The Bible's Good News about Living a Generous Life* (Eerdmans, 2006).

 Notes